How to F

MW01257475

the Backyard

A Duck Farming Guide for Beginners

David Josephson

No part of this publication may be reproduced, or transmitted in any form or by any means including photocopying, recording or other electronics or mechanical method without the prior permission of the publisher except for brief quotations embodied in critical reviews.

Table of Contents

About this Book

This insightful book covers all aspects of backyard duck raising from selecting a breed and buying ducks to housing, feeding, and health. It includes a description of the common breed suitable for any backyard. The peculiarity of each breed, their egg-laying capacity and their potential as table birds are critically examined. It also contains a comprehensive section on incubation of eggs both natural and artificial methods. You will also learn how to protect your flocks from predators.

Backyard duck homesteaders and hobby farmers will find this book an enjoyable and useful resource; it will make your duck raising adventure a profitable experience.

Introduction

Raising ducks in the backyard is a wonderful experience; ducks are delightful and bring a lot of entertainment to the yard. If you are looking for a profitable addition to a backyard flock, or just a fun companion to provide viable meat and entertainment, ducks certainly fill the gap. People all over the world like duck meat and egg from the ancient time. Ducks can be raised in small spaces without specialized equipment, a large budget or extensive experience; they can be maintained with minimal equipment and expenses. In addition, they represent an excellent prospect of making extra income. Duck eggs are a special product favorite among bakers and chefs who prize them for their rich flavor. Duck meat can be raised and sold for a seasonal market, or only produced for family needs. Also, you can generate additional income selling ducklings.

1 Benefits of Raising Ducks

Raising ducks in the backyard brings a lot of benefits and pleasure. Caring for duck is relatively easier compared to chickens, they appear to be smarter and have more personality than chickens. They are more comfortable to keep confined in pens and appear more proficient layers. They can lay up to 350 eggs a year weighing five to eight ounces per dozen more than chicken eggs. Practical experience and tests conducted by institutions show that duck eggs retain their freshness during storage considerably longer than those of chickens. Furthermore, they produce longer than a chicken, well into a fifth or even sixth season.

Ducks naturally run a feverishly high temperature which makes them resistant to most diseases. They are hardier than chickens, both as babies and as adults. When fully feathered, their body is weatherproof which keep them warm and dry. Their waterproof down coats keep them warm and dry – and happy – in even the worst of weather. On the wet, dreary days, your ducks will make you smile with their cheerful, puddle-splashing antics. They do fine in both cold and hot weather, too, as long as they have access to shade and bathing water.

Biological Control of Pests

Ducks can be used as a biological control of insect pests in rice and grain farming. This is a common practice in many parts of Southeast Asia where duck

Benefits of Raising Ducks

production has been integrated with rice and fish farming. They range freely eating slugs, snails, and insect pests in the field. They also eat slugs, snails, clean algae slime and duckweed from ponds, thereby eliminating mosquito larvae from waterways. Given the opportunity, they will also feast on small snakes, toads and even mice.

Ducks are generally healthier. They seem to be far less susceptible to mites and other external parasites than chickens because they spend reasonable time in the water. Any external parasites that might be tempted to latch on will drown.

They are so fun to watch! Chickens are pleasant and fantastic to watch as they peck around the yard or flap in their dirt baths, but ducks are completely amusing! They are social. Watching them interact with each other is exciting; they are very expressive with their body language and love to "talk" to each other. It is entertaining watching them swim and dive in a pool. There is something just so endearing and pure about how cheerful they get when you fill the pool with fresh water.

2. Understanding Backyard Duck Behavior

Ducks are intelligent birds with complex social relationships. Understanding their needs is crucial before jumping into raising them. Here are a few thoughts to know and consider before adding a group of ducks to your yard. Ducks live in both fresh and seawater and can be found on every continent except for Antarctica.Duck Terms

Term	Meaning
Duckling	A baby duck
Drake	Drake
Hen or duck	A female duck
A raft	A group of ducks, a team or a paddling

Understanidng Backyard Duck Behavior

Generic "bird" terms can also be used like chick, bird or flock.

Amazing Facts

Ducks can sleep with one eye open −if Ducks feel unsafe in any environment, they can sleep keeping one eye open. Duck's brains are split in half with one half controlling one eye and the other half controlling the other eye. They sleep to turn off half their brain while keeping the other half alert for emergencies such as predators attack. Ducks will usually only fully rest both halves when they feel secure either in the middle of a large group of ducks or in a safe place.

Waterproofing

Ducks feathers are waterproof. They can dive wholly underwater, and the downy under-feathers will stay dry. They have a unique feather pattern and a wax-like coating that they spread onto their feathers while preening. The waxy oil is produced in their preen gland, a small gland at the base of their tail. Also, ducks have a particular countercurrent blood vessel system in their feet so their feet will not feel cold. This feature enables them to swim in icy water and be undisturbed by walking in snow & chilly puddles and also free from frostbite

Molting

Molting is a common occurrence with most birds. During this period they lose their flight feathers one at a time. Ducks molting starts typically in spring or early summer, where they lose all their primary feathers at once. This means they can't fly until they grow back their feathers about 20-40 days. The good thing is that they are well adapted to flightless life by inhabiting wetlands where they don't need to fly to get food and shelter.

Mating

Drakes are among the few bird species that have an external phallus. It is long and corkscrew shaped to fit inside the female's twisting and turning vaginal canal. It draws back into their body when not in a mating position. The process of duck mating can be pretty harsh and aggressive that can sometimes even result in injury or death. The female flattens out, and the male climbs on her back. He grabs the back of her head with his bill to help him balance. In some species of ducks, a female will tie with a male for one season. When harassed into mating by other drakes, she will keep the sperm and eject it later, so that she only reproduces with the male of her choosing partner. Preen after swimming- Ducks engage in elaborate preening of their feathers after swimming. They rub their heads all over their body to distribute their natural oils on their feathers that help keep them waterproof. At the base of the tail, there is a small preening gland that they stimulate to release the oils.

Head bobbing-They Bob their head up and down. When they get some tasty treats, see a duck friend they haven't seen sometimes, or when their pool is fresh and clean, they bob their head in excitement.

The Right Breed

There are various duck breeds available throughout the world. Not all of these breeds are suitable for backyard duck farming. For best results, it is essential to choose a breed that best suits your particular needs. Obtain stock from a supplier who breeds selectively for the qualities you want.

Sociability

Ducks are very sociable creatures; you should have it in mind to keep more than just one duck. Keeping at least two will ensure they stay happy.

Consider Your Space

Ducks, unlike chickens, don't bear confinement well they do need a good portion of land to range and graze. You can't merely keep and restrict ducks in a coop-and-run combo in the corner of your yard. Ducks should have access to a decent-sized body of water not just to drink, but to swim in, eat in, bathe in, poop in. You should consider providing your ducks with an artificial pond or use your home swimming pool to keep your ducks cool.

Consider Keeping Males

For your ducks to start breeding, you should consider adding a drake. They are quieter than the females, unlike chicken roosters One drake is good enough for almost 5 to 6 ducks.

Eating and Drinking

Ducks loves water, they can't have food without water. They usually dip their food in water to make it digestible. If they were to feed without having water to go with it, the feed would stay in their crop, and when they drink again, the food will swell up and possibly choke them.

Cleaning and Maintenance

Ducks cleaning and maintenance requires a bit more work compared with other domesticated birds. You have to keep them in clean water always. They poop a lot. They will dirty their pool and try to swim in any available water including their water bowls thereby creating a muddy environment. Causing splash it requires continuous attention to maintain a hygienic environment. Ducks poop is messy and smelly, and they poop a lot. The good thing is that it is soft and watery, unlike chicken mess. It lacks the burning intensity of chicken manure and doesn't need to be composted to soft. Water from ducks pond is rich in manure, using that for a garden can be a great way to hit your garden with some excellent nutrition.

3 Duck House Plans Guide

Ducks don't need much in terms of housing. They don't need anything fancy. What they need is a secure, safe place to retreat to. Ducks are amazingly resistant to cold and wet weather. They can be kept in a simple shed-like structure and does not need elaborate furniture such as raised nests and dropping pits. They don't need perches either because they roost on the ground at night. If you intend housing your ducks only at night, a minimum of three to five square feet of floor space per duck is required. During severe weather, if you need keeping your ducks inside continuously, you should consider providing each bird with 8 to 15 per square feet. This helps keep bedding reasonably dry and hygienic.

You can keep them in a wooden box or old dog house that is at least 3 feet high, with 4 square feet of floor space for each duck you plan to have.

The house should either be on the ground or have a low ramp which can be placed off a corner of your barn. You can even house them in your chicken coop if you want to. Ensure that the duck house is suitable, safe and comfortable for living with your ducks.

Some Other Things to Consider

Keeping these various points in mind will help you to build a simple house or convert an existing structure into a safe, secure house for your ducks.

- Ducks are vulnerable to predators because they roost on the ground. At night, they should be properly locked up in a yard that is tightly fenced. You needs to put a predator-proof latch on it (remember that a determined coyote and racoons can slide deadbolts and lift locks).

• Size. Ducks need enough room to get comfortable. You should consider 4 square feet of floor space per duck

Flooring. You can place Duck houses directly on the ground but should have a wooden or cement floor to prevent predators from digging underneath to gain access.

• Bedding. Straw and Pine shavings work well for bedding. Straw has wonderful insulating properties during extremely cold weather, keeping ducks warm;

it also holds its shape better, so they don't end up sleeping on the cold wood or cement floor.

• Nesting Boxes. Ducks hardly ever use nesting boxes. But, if you wish to include some boxes, they should be at floor level. The boxes should be at least 13- 14 square inches and filled with clean straw.

• Ventilation. The most important thing the duck house needs is ventilation. Make sure the house is well ventilated. Ducks release lots of moisture when they breathe, and if that moisture can't escape, it can cause health problems. It can lead to moldy and mildewed bedding or even frostbitten legs and feet in winter. The house should be spacious and tall enough to accommodate vents along the top close to the roof for air flow. Also, the house should also include additional windows. All vents and windows should be well covered with 1/2-inch hardware cloth to prevent predators from gaining access.

Water

Water is critical to ducks existence they love water. Making water available for swimming is not a must (Ducks do not need bathing water to remain healthy), but it will make your ducks happy. However, it is essential they have access to fresh, clean water. Ducks need steady access to fresh water for drinking, for mixing with their food and for keeping their nostrils moist. High-producing ducks need a steady supply of reasonably clean drinking water. Adult ducks need as much as half a gallon of water a day. Both the number and size of eggs will suffer if birds are frequently allowed to go thirsty. Water containers do not need to be elaborate but should be deep enough that the duckling can dip their entire head in the water. Four to six inches deep water level is okay to permit the ducks to clean their bills and eyes. Abandoned equipment such as a child's wading pool or an old hot water tank that has been cut in half can be converted for bathing by ducks.

Lighting

Day length is extremely important to laying birds. It affects the reproductive organs of poultry. For steady egg production during winter ducks like chickens, must be exposed to a minimum of 13 to 14 hours of light daily. Therefore, during the short days between September and April, laying ducks need supplemental lighting in most areas of the Northern Hemisphere.

4. Choosing the Right Duck Breed

There are various duck breeds available throughout the world, but not all are suitable for backyard duck farming. For best results, it is important to choose a breed that best suits your particular needs. Obtain stock from a supplier who breeds selectively for the qualities you want. Ducks have been genetically developed for special purposes, mainly meat production and egg production. In addition, ducks are raised for an exhibition, pest control, and feather and down production.

Generally, Duck breeds are categorized into four different classes—heavy, medium, lightweight, and bantam.

Meat Duck Breeds

Heavy and medium weight ducks are raised mainly for meat production. The meat breed of choice in many areas include   Peking, Ayleshbari, Maskovi, Ruel Kagua and the Swiden.

Egg Duck Breeds

The runner and Campbell breeds are exceptional egg producers , often attaining levels of production higher than those of egg-laying chicken breeds.

In making your choice there are specific characteristics to look for especially if you are a beginner with little or no experience.

Choosing the Right Duck Breed

You need to choose a breed that is friendly and easy to care for.If your purpose is egg production, look for a high egg producing breed. If your purpose is meat production, you need the one that gains weight quickly.

Next, we want to examine some common breeds and their characteristics.

Mallard

Mallards are thought to be the "father" of all domestic ducks except for Muscovy. They are small duck breed, making them capable of flight. Most people that keep Mallards do so for purely decorative reasons, or for training hunting dogs. Their egg laying ability is poor, laying just a couple of greenish eggs per week. They are incredibly energetic and talkative. Male and female ducks look similar with male ducks having a shiny green head with a white ring around their neck and grey on their wings and belly, while the females are mainly brown-speckled with a blue band on their wing.

Pekin

Pekin ducks are vast foragers and are also a friendly breed. They are considered a general purpose breed- they are a great meat source and layers of large white eggs. Most duck meat produced in the United States is from the Pekin. A Pekin usually reaches 6 to 7 pounds in seven or eight weeks and 7 to 8 pounds under intensive care.

Choosing the Right Duck Breed

Muscovy

Muscovy is an exciting bird native to the southern hemisphere. They are usually raised as a broody and a meat duck breed. The Meat of the Muscovy duck is of fine quality and good taste. They are also gaining popularity as backyard pets and exhibition birds. The Muscovy ducks are a somewhat unique bird they usually do not swim as much as other breeds because their oil glands are underdeveloped so you don't need a large volume of water for raising them. They are usually gentle birds unless the duck is brooding or tending duckling. The drakes are not noisy and don't quack as well, instead have a low hiss or breathy call. They are the quietest of all the domesticated duck breeds. The Muscovy ducks are good at flying; they need to be wing-clipped. The ducks can fly long distances. But the drakes are less flighty mainly because of their weight. Drakes are much more massive than the ducks. The Muscovy ducks usually roost in small groups in trees like chickens. The ducks are fair egg layers but are excellent brooders. Some people appreciate these breeds for their distinctive appearance, intelligence and friendly and trusting personality

Khaki Campbells

Khaki Campbells are another highly recommended duck breed. They are excellent foragers with excellent egg laying abilities. They can lay up to 5-6 cream colored eggs per week! Their excellent egg laying abilities make them one of the most popular choices for backyard keepers. They are smaller in size usually weighing about 3 pounds but have limited flight ability- they can fly for limited distances. Campbells are a warm khaki color bird. Their feet color differs by sex. The drakes have orange feet with a darker bronze colored tail, while the females have brown feet.

Buff Orpington

Buff Orpington Duck is a dual-purpose breed used for meat and egg production. It is capable of laying an average of 3-5 white to light brown eggs per week. The Orpington duck was initially created by the famous poultry breeder 'William Cook' of Orpington, Kent, England in the early 1900s. William Cook was also the developer of the Orpington chicken. The breed is available in three colour varieties which usually appear from the offspring; Buff, Blond and Brown. They have lovely fawn buff feathers with a brownish orange bill. Both male and female Orpington have brown eyes, orange-yellow shanks and feet, and buff plumage, but their bill differs in color. The duck's bill is brown-orange, while the drake's bill is yellow. The Orpington duck is considered a threatened duck breed by the American Livestock Breeds Conservancy.

Cayugas

Cayugas originated near Cayuga Lake in New York in the United States. They are usually raised for ornament/exhibition or eggs purposes. Their calm disposition makes them a great choice for backyard flocks.

They are black with a green head. The Cayuga breed is in the Medium Class, an average adult male weighs is 8 pounds and females 7 pounds. They are characterized by a black bill and black iridescent feathers that can look green in certain light. The females are quite vocal while often the male is mute. The temperament of the Cayuga is docile, and adult Cayuga Ducks enjoy eating snails, slugs, and most other insects. They lay 3-4 eggs per week and have charcoal or grey/black colored shell and will more often sit on and hatch her eggs than other domestic breeds of duck.

Aylesbury duck

The Aylesbury duck is a breed of domestic duck, which is named after the place of its creation like the

Orpington duck, it was created in the United Kingdom, developed around the early eighteenth Century from the town of Aylesbury in Buckinghamshire, it is a breed of domesticated duck, raised mostly for its meat and appearance.

The Aylesbury duck is a large duck with pure white plumage orange legs and feet, a long pink bill and a horizontal stance. The pins are placed midway along the body, and it stands with its underside parallel to the ground, giving it a body which is usually described as "boat-shaped". ". They have relatively long and thin swan-like neck. Their eyes are of dark greyish blue color aylesbury ducks are of two types; exhibition and utility. The exhibition type has a very deep keel which makes it difficult for them to mate naturally. The utility type has a relatively smaller keel and can mate naturally successfully. By one year of age, females and males grow to an average weight of 2.7 and 3.2 kg respectively, although drakes can reach around 5 kg.

Rouen

Rouen is mainly kept as a general purpose duck. Their larger size makes them suitable for raising as a meat duck. And they are also very ideal for exhibition or ornamental purpose. They are relatively quiet and very easy to tame and a good alternative to Mallards because of their seemingly identical nature. The Rouen ducks are considered as an excellent waterfowl for the ranch pond and a good choice as backyard ducks. They are sociable, good foragers and good for pest controller. They are pretty slow maturing breed and can take a year for achieving full size. Although they produce high-quality meat, they are not among the best egg laying duck breeds, averaging about 150 large white eggs per year.

That's why they may not be suitable for commercial duck farming business. But they have great demand in the market for quality meat because they produce leaner meat than the Pekin duck.

Saxony

Saxony duck bred initially in the 1930s in Germany is a great dual-purpose breed, suitable for both meat and eggs production and adapt well to a wide range of environments the Saxony is a heavy, fast-growing duck who also lays a large amount of white or light blue eggs up to 200 per year. The ducks are broody and will sit on the eggs until they hatch. They are

relatively gentle birds, fairly easy going, have a calm temperament instead and are not flyers, although, the females are quite noisy. In addition, they are beautiful birds and well suited to both watching and petting. They usually do not quack. Instead, they make a raspy sound if anyhow they become excited. Their colors are unique from any other breed although Males display the characteristic Mallard pattern. The drake's head and wing markings are blue-grey, with a chestnut breast and cream belly.

Ancona

Ancona ducks are among the good egg layers of all domesticated duck breeds. They are mainly raised for eggs production. But as they are dual purpose utility duck breed, so they are also suitable for meat production. They are very hardy and adaptable water bird. They are not flighty and pretty calm birds and would be a good choice for pond and backyard farming. They are good as pets and like to stay close to home if handled form very young age. Usually, the Ancona lays for 5-8 years with the peak period in the first three years. Eggs become increasingly bigger as the birds get older. Ancona ducks grow at a faster rate and produce high-quality meat which is more flavorful and less fatty than that of the most Pekin ducks.

Choosing the Right Duck Breed

They are vast foragers and can arrange their diet with greens, bugs, slugs, insects and other arthropods if allowed to forage freely in the backyard.

Magpie

Magpie – A lightweight bird, created for general purpose breed. They are good layers and also good as a meat duck breed. The Magpie ducks are excellent foragers who will graze and hunt for a sizable portion of their feed from grass, seeds, insects and snails. They are large egg laying breed – laying 4-5 colorful eggs per week. Magpie's eggs can vary from white, cream, blue and green. They are mainly found black & white, but also be blue & white with an orange bill. The breed is generally a quiet and calm, hardy, strong and long-lived. The lifespan of an average Magpie duck is between 9 and 12 years. They can also be raised for an exhibition.

5. How to Raise Ducklings

Raising ducklings is almost much the same with raising chickens. Much of the information applicable to raising baby chicken can be applied to ducks, as long as the significant differences between these two species are taken into account.

For the first few weeks, it is essential to have your ducklings in a brooder situated in a climate controlled environment like a spare bedroom, stock tank, swimming pool, bath top or laundry room in your home. Also, you will need a few supplies and items.

The list includes the following;

You'll be using a heat lamp with a reflector to regulate the temperature of the brooder.

Bedding materials; pine shavings, straw and hay or other soft materials.

Feed starter pack which can be obtained from feed supply stores; this is what they need at the initial stage.

A waterer and the feeder

A thermometer

The Brooder

The ducklings first home is the brooder. The size of the brooder depends on the number of ducklings you have in mind but ideally use at least 2.5-3 squares feet per duckling is okay. Set up the brooder in a clean space, draft-free, protected from predators. Using the bathtub works well because the bathroom door can be securely shut to keep the ducklings safe from any intruder. It seems to be the most effective method in containing their mess. Ducklings are messy, they will play in their water, and the brooder will be soaking wet all the time no matter what you do.

When your ducklings arrive home, before setting them into the prepared pre-heated brooder, dip each duckling's bill into a shallow dish of room-temperature water. Keep the temperature at 90 degrees for the first week, then reduce a degree a day for a total of 7 degrees per week. Do this until they are feathered out, and the brooder temp is the same as the room temperature. Then you can transfer the duckling to a predator-proof house/pen. By the time they are 3-5 weeks old, weather-dependent, they can spend warm, sunny days outside, carefully supervised.

How to know if too Hot or too Cold with your baby ducks.

Until the baby ducks are completely feathered around 7-9 weeks old, they have trouble regulating their body temperature and need heat. You need to observe them to know the situation and the action to take.

If they cluster near the heat source, then it's too cold you need to increase the effect of the heat.

Conversely, if they stay away from the heat lamp, they are too hot you have to reduce the effects of the heat.

If they are dull, lie down in a corner and pant a lot; that is also a sign that they are too hot.

Ducklings hatched in an incubator, unlike those hatched naturally; don't have oil glands working yet. Their oil glands will not be fully working to coat and waterproof their feathers until they are older. They can easily become soaked or drown if exposed to too much water. Therefore, a shallow water bowl which they can submerge their entire bill to keep their mucous membranes moist should be provided for water. Once they are about 5-6 weeks old, you can let them play in the water a little. You should expose them to short, supervised swims. You can fill a plastic tub with warm water and allow them to splash around for a few minutes to get them used to be in the water.

Water

Drinking water must be available at all times. Ducks drink a lot. They cannot swallow their food without water, so they need it close by especially at feeding times.

A week-old baby duck will drink up to half a gallon of water a week. By the time they are seven weeks old, they drink a half gallon of water a day, so be sure their water is always filled.

Ducks like to rake their beaks through their bedding and their water. They will get their water everywhere- on themselves, on their food, on their bedding.

6. What to Feed Ducks

Ducks have a higher protein and energy requirements. What they eat affects their health, growth, and production. They need foods that provide the nutrients, minerals, and vitamins required for healthy growth and development.

They are excellent foragers. They forage for insects, snails, worms, especially near water area where they can find aquatic insects when dabbling through the water or mud. While free-ranging on grass, they will also consume seed heads as well as small amounts of grass, chickweed and clover.

Wild ducks will find most of their food and fend for themselves and can survive independently. However domestic ducks that are bred to lay more eggs and restricted to a smaller area can't survive without extra feed. They require a balanced feed for optimum production. There is waterfowl feed available commercially. They can do quite well on chicken feed as well.

Commercial Feed

Commercial feed is perfectly formulated to provide the nutrients, minerals, and vitamins the birds need for healthy growth and development it is a mix of grains, chemicals, minerals, and vitamins. There are various mixes such as layer feed, chick starter, grower feed, and broiler finisher. The variety you can choose from depends on the age of your flock.

What to Feed Ducks

Grains

Grain choices include corn, wheat, oats, sorghum, barley, spelt, rye, triticale, buckwheat, amaranth, and more. Grains are an excellent choice, but you cannot depend on it alone to feed your flocks as they don't have all the nutrition ducks need especially protein. Laying ducks need a diet with approximately 17% protein which is not contained in grains. The only way you could feed your birds only grain would be if they find most of their food through free-ranging.

Vegetables and Fruits

Vegetables and fruits can be an excellent supplement to your ducks' diet! Some food leftovers are okay to feed your flocks, such as salad or rice and veggies such as wilted cabbage, lettuce, tomatoes and bananas, and Cucumber

Grits

Just like chickens, ducks do need grits to help them digest their food. Foraging allows them to pick up enough small stones, pebbles, and coarse dirt to satisfy their grit need. If you don't let your ducks out to roam you have to provide them commercial grit.

Meat

Ducks are omnivores. They feed on meat! They love fish and egg. Often, while roaming, If they have access to the pond they will catch small fish as well as eat the fish eggs. They gobble up slugs, worms, snails, even lizards and tiny frogs.

What to Feed Ducks

Here are your feeding options:

If your ducks have access to a significant amount of foraging space, you should opt for natural feeding! Feed them bits from your garden, give them some raw grains, and if that's not enough, supplement with some commercial feed. Your ducks will be happy, healthy, and relatively cheap to feed and maintain.

Tips for Feeding Ducks

•   Stop feeding if you notice that the birds no longer respond and are leaving the food uneaten since leftover food can quickly rot and attract unwanted pests

•   Don't overfeed as too much food can lead to health problems and wastages

• Ducks do not chew. Therefore offer foods in bite-sized pieces the birds can easily consume without choking or struggling.

• Litter can hurt your ducks in many ways, so be sure to dispose of all trash properly, including twist ties, plastic clips, and any unsuitable or moldy scraps

• Be sure your ducks have fresh water and grit to help them digest the food.

• Treats for your ducks should not be more than 10% of their daily diet, although green treats, such as chard, lettuce, etc. can be fed in unlimited quantity.

After hatching and brooding ducklings, your ducklings will need chick starter which contains about 20% protein and chicken grower feed 16%

protein, as well as lots of water. Once your ducklings approach adult ducks size, the way you go about feeding your ducks change.

Feeding Baby Ducks

Early Duckling Stage (0-2 weeks)

Ducks can be started on regular chick starter feed if waterfowl feed is not available. They need higher protein at this early growth period. To facilitate fast growth, make sure you are providing your ducklings with enough protein. Look for a high protein chick starter (20-22% would be ideal) for those first two weeks. Unlike chicks who stay on the starter feed for the first eight weeks, ducklings should only be on it for the first two weeks after hatching. It is advisable to choose the unmedicated chick starter feed.

Because ducklings eat so much more than chicks, so that they don't over medicate themselves. Chick feed is medicated to prevent coccidiosis, which is common among chickens in the early stage, ducks are not susceptible to coccidiosis.

Other things to consider with feeding ducklings chick starter is the niacin levels. Niacin requirement varies, baby ducks require more amount of niacin than chicks, deficiencies can lead to bowed legs and joint issues. .Adding some brewer's yeast to the feed will provide niacin for strong bones. Powdered brewer's yeast is a good source of niacin. Mix 1.5 tablespoons of brewers yeast to every cup of chick feed to supply the nutrient. Always make available plenty of fresh water with the feed. They need plenty of water to help digest their food and keep off on additional treats at this time.

Later Duckling Stage (3-20 weeks)

Ducks grow fast after two weeks; the ducklings should be switched to chicken grower feed which has lower protein content. High protein diet can lead to issues such as Angel Wing which is caused by too much protein in the menu. To avoid a protein overload, switch to a lower protein chick starter feed (16-18% protein, non medicated feed). If a lower protein feed is not available, you can mix your starter feed with rolled oats. Mix in rolled oats, up to a 25 per cent ratio to the feed. Also, continue to supplement with brewer's yeast until about 20 weeks to take care of niacin requirement, at this stage you can start to introduce treats to their diet gradually. Remember always to provide plenty of fresh water.

Adult Ducks (21 weeks+)

At this point, the duck is just about full grown and will be getting ready to lay her first egg. Your ducks can be switched to layer feed(chicken or waterfowl layer feed) which has the added calcium they need to lay eggs with strong shells. You don't need to supplement with the brewer's yeast anymore. Duck eggs are larger and have thicker shells than chicken eggs, so the appropriate calcium levels are essential. The feed should contain at least 16% protein and added calcium to help form thicker eggshells. You should also add crushed eggshell or oyster shell free choice in addition to the layer feed. If all your ducks are older and no longer laying, or if you are keeping drakes only, you should use a maintenance diet lower in protein (about 14%) and calcium.

Feed (crumble or pellet) should be offered free choice throughout the day along with access to plenty of fresh, clean water. An adult duck needs up to a half gallon of water every day. The feed bowl should be cleaned daily, because ducks like to moisten their feed. Wet food can become moldy which is not suitable for your birds

Treats

Chickens and ducks enjoy similar treats. Ducklings can also eat a variety of healthy treats, as long as they are cut into small pieces or are soft or mushy to prevent choking.

Treats for your ducks should not be more than 10% of their daily diet, although green treats, such as chard, lettuce, etc. can be fed in unlimited amounts.

The following healthy treats can be offered free choice along with their feed:

- Cracked corn. Crushed eggshell,

- Wheat, barley, or similar grains.

- Oats (uncooked; rolled or quick)

- lettuce/greens

- Rice (cooked or uncooked)

- Milo seed.

- Birdseed (any type or mix)

What Ducks Shouldn't Eat

Don't feed your ducks bread. It has very little in the way of vitamins and minerals that a duck needs to be healthy. Feeding ducks with a diet which contains mainly bread, or bread-like products such as cookies, popcorn and doughnuts, will lead to excessive weight gain that causes obesity. It can also lead to other health problems such as malnutrition and poor development. Also, it can also lead to impacted crops which can be fatal for your birds. However, whole grain pieces of bread may not be harmful, if given in limited quantity with plenty of fresh water.

Avoid giving your birds Citrus fruits such as lemons, limes, grapefruit, oranges. They can cause acid reflux and stomach pain in ducks. They are also thought to interfere with calcium absorption and contribute to thin-shelled eggs.

Spinach should be fed only in limited amounts. It is claimed to interfere with calcium absorption, a situation which can cause egg binding or soft-shelled eggs. Others vegetable to avoid include Iceberg lettuce, white potatoes rhubarb, green tomatoes and eggplant.

Ducks don't digest nuts and large seeds properly, since they swallow their food whole Nuts and seeds can also cause choking or get stuck in the crop. If you do feed nuts or seeds to your ducks, they should be grinded first.

7. Managing Ducks for Egg Production

Ducks don't always lay in a nest and will usually lay very early in the morning or sometimes through the night. Try to collect the eggs as soon as possible to lessens the problems of dirty and cracked eggs. For quality egg production, you have to manage your flock well and take good care of them. Soiled eggs can be washed with care after collection using warm water.

Caring For Laying Ducks

Egg production is greatly influenced by the quality of food that a laying duck is eating. Therefore, it is essential to feed a laying duck with a diet that is well balanced in the nutrients necessary to maintain good reproductive performance. Using a diet feed containing sufficient amount of required vitamins and minerals is crucial. Generally, an egg-laying duck will consume approximately 6 to 8 ounces of feed daily. In addition, always make available a sufficient amount of clean and fresh water to your duck.

Lighting

Ducks ability to produce eggs is generally dependent on how much light is present during the day. Appropriate lighting is another important consideration. Ducks can be brought into full production by exposing them to 14 hours of light daily. When the days become shortened, artificial light can be added to the day by using a 40 to 60 watt light bulb in the coop. Similarly, decrease the amount of using artificial light when the sun stays for a long time.

Ducks start egg production when they reach sexual maturity at about seven months of age. If you need fertilized duck's eggs, then you need to keep one drake for every 5 to 6 laying ducks. This is crucial to prevent aggression and injury. Check the bedding of your laying ducks daily and ensure that it is always clean and dry.

Hatching Duck Eggs

Eggs from common ducks such as Pekins take about 28 days to hatch while Muscovy ducks take about 35 days. Carefully select the eggs to be set in the setting trays. Do not set cracked, double yolked, misshapen, abnormally small, oversized, undersized or dirty eggs. Hatching eggs can be stored for up to two weeks at a temp of 55 degrees F. without losing hatchability, but for best results, set eggs within 1-3 days from laying period. Eggs should be set small end down. On the day of setting make sure the incubator is working correctly, Close the doors and allow the incubator to reach operating temperature before setting the eggs. Set ventilation and temperature as recommended by the incubator manufacturer. Eggs must be turned at least 4 times a day either automatically or manually. Most automatic turning devices are set to turn the eggs hourly.

Check frequently to ensure that things are in order. At about seven days after setting, candle the eggs and remove any eggs that are infertile.

At 25 days after setting (Pekin eggs), candle and remove eggs with dead embryos and transfer the eggs to hatching trays where they will remain to hatch on the 28th day. The temperature of the hatcher should be set at 99°F. As the process near completion gradually lower the temperature and humidity so that by the end of the procedure the temperature is at 97°F. You can remove ducklings from the hatcher when about 90-95% of them are dry.

Natural Incubation

Ducks can hatch their eggs naturally. Some of them are excellent setters, capable of hatching 12-15 eggs.

Provide clean, dry nesting facilities. Ducks can even make their own nest if they have access to straw or other litter material. Feed and water should be nearby for the broody duck so she can obtain her daily nutrient requirements without having to leave the nest for long brooding periods.

8. A Guide to Common Duck Diseases

Ducks are generally incredibly resistant to disease. They are extremely strong and don't often get sick as long as they are well fed and adequately maintained. Providing healthy diet, plenty of fresh, dry feed, giving them lots of clean water to drink and swim in, and keeping their house and yard clean is the easiest way to have healthy, happy ducks. They are generally healthy and hardy. In addition, they aren't quite as vulnerable to external parasites as chickens do because they spend considerable time in the water which drowns any threatening parasite such as ticks, lice and mites. But even healthy ducks can sometimes get sick, or get injured.

Most ducks problems are often traceable to diet deficiencies, poor drinking water or dirty bedding. High-quality preventatives and proper duck yard sanitation go a long way towards raising a healthy happy flock.

Here are some fairly common duck diseases that you should be aware of if you raise backyard ducks.

Bumble foot

Bumble foot, is a staphylococcus infection caused by a cut, hard landing or splinter. It is a disease common to both chickens and ducks. The virus usually begins a cut on the underside of the foot and as the bird walks around in mud, dirt and poop the cut can get infected. The infection can eventually lead to blood poisoning and death if not treated. You can treat the disease by soaking the bird's foot in warm water to loosen the kernel that forms around the infection. After removing the kernel successfully, you can treat the area with Neosporin and covered with a gauze pad & Vetrap and changed daily to keep the foot clean and dry. To prevent the disease make sure to keep the duck pen free of sharp stones, branches and other harmful objects. Also, check the bottom of your duck's feet occasionally to detect sores or other duck foot problems.

Eye Infection

Symptoms of an eye infection include a closed eye, foamy eye, redness or tearing. Debris, a scratch or rough mating can all cause eye irritation in ducks. If your duck develops eye irritations, rinse her eyes twice a day with saline solution and provide clean water deep enough for them to dip their whole head in so they can keep their mucous membranes moist. This exercise often clears up the problem, but if it persists in a few days, a compress of steeped chamomile tea or goldenseal can help clear up the irritation.

Respiratory Issues

Respiratory issues in ducks can arise sometimes hand in hand with eye problems,   Separating the affected bird quickly will hopefully stop the spread. Boost her immune system by adding electrolytes to her water can also help. You can also aid her breathing by putting a few drops of Vet Rx under her wing in the night, as she tucks in to sleep the smell will help clear up congestion.

Botulism

Botulism thrives in decaying waste or pools of water and common in warm weather. Botulism is a serious disease which can cause death within hours. It is important to keep water sources clean regularly. You can use white vinegar and a scrub brush on the water tubs and pool regularly to keep it sanitized.

Impacted Crop

Ducks sometimes suffer impacted crop if they ingest long pieces of string, twine, plastic or any foreign objects which get lodged in the upper part of the digestive system (the crop). The throat area may look swollen or feel hard. If you suspect impacted crop in your duck, gently massage the area, then offer grit, some olive oil and plenty of water to break up the mass and allow it to pass. Ducks will eat practically anything they can get hold of in the yard. Be sure to keep the roam area free from any potentially dangerous materials. Also, if you are to feed ducks cut grass or weeds, make sure they are cut into fairly short lengths.

Prolapsed Penis/Vent

A prolapse occurs in ducks when a part of the oviduct pushes outside the duck's body while laying an egg. In drakes, it happens when the penis doesn't retract after mating. The situation can correct itself in both cases. It's a good idea to separate the affected bird to prevent mating while the prolapse is healing.

Furthermore, keep the area clean, and apply some coconut oil and sugar for a few days to tighten the skin tissue and keep it soft. If after some days there is no improvement you can carefully push the prolapse back inside. A healthy diet can help prevent prolapses in your flock. In severe cases, a visit to the vet might be in order.

Angel Wing

Angel Wing is caused by overfeeding high protein food. It is a non-life threatening condition. The wing grows too fast and doesn't lie flat against the body. The situation can be normalized by reducing the protein content of their feed. Provide plenty of exercises and putting the wing in a sling.

Aspergillosis

Aspergillosis is caused by fungal spores. It causes intense, strenuous breathing in ducks. The situation can be prevented by removing wet feed and bedding promptly.

Wry Neck

Wryneck is a condition in which a duckling is unable to hold its head up and will often not be able to walk correctly. It can be caused in ducklings by a vitamin deficiency, blow to the head or ingestion of toxins. It can be fatal if not treated in good time. You can supplement their diet with vitamin capsules, or add some brewer's yeast, bran, sunflower seeds or wheat germ to reverse the condition.

A Guide to Common Duck Diseases

Wet Feather

Wet feather is a condition where ducks preen gland, which keeps their feathers well-oiled and waterproofed, stops working. This condition usually occurs when ducks are kept in poor sanitary condition or not allowed regular access to water in which to swim. The disease manifests with duck not being able to stay dry in the rain or water and seems not to be waterproof anymore. Remove the dirt by bathing her in dawn detergent, then rinse her well and blow dry her to give her the chance to start all over. Extreme cases often require the duck to go through a molt and develop new feathers before she is normal and waterproof again.

Soft Shelled eggs

Ducks that lay too many eggs are prone to laying eggs with defects-soft shells, small holes or no shells. It can be an indication that your duck lacks calcium in his diet. Adding calcium to their diet will help. This can be given in the form of ground oyster shells, or other calcium supplements. The calcium helps keep the shells thick and strong.. Another alternative is to mix raw black sesame seeds with their food. Ground old egg shells and fresh leafy greens are a natural source of calcium. Sesame is a good natural source of calcium, zinc, fibre, vitamin B1, magnesium and phosphorous.

9. How to Protect Ducks from Predators

Ducks are fantastic birds almost any wild creature, and many domestic ones can appreciate delicious duck meat. It is, therefore, possible to lose your pet to predation occasionally. With rapid urbanization and other human activities, more wild-life are entering urban settings a development which is not too good for urban farmers. Predators can come in all forms and shapes and are active both during the day and night. They can attack your flock from the sky, at ground level or by digging underground. Types of predators that might attack your flock vary depending on your location. Therefore, it is necessary for you to know what predators your flock might be facing in your area. Some predators are after ducks meat, while some are after eggs and sometimes both. Some of these predators are very smart, others opportunists. The good thing is that each can be deterred by a simple security measure. Once you know which predators are likely to attack your flock, then you can create an effective defense system to stop their obnoxious activities.

Land predators

Common land predators include foxes, coyotes, raccoons, snakes, bears, weasels, fisher cats, bobcats, and badgers others are wolves and minks. It is also possible for ducks to be attacked by feral cats or even the domestic dog.

How to Protect Ducks from Predators

Aerial predators

Common aerial predators otherwise known as birds of prey include Hawks, Owls, and Eagles.

The long-term solution for protecting your flock is to prevent these invaders from gaining access to your flock. Be ready to take swift action if you discover any predation. Your Failure to act on time will result in subsequent visit and losses. If predators feel they have an easy catch available in your yard, they will keep visiting to cause more tremendous damages.

Coop Security

The first step is to have a secure coop with a door that shuts firmly at night. Use sturdy mesh for fencing and not chicken wire and ensure that your coop is sturdy and predator-proof. Check regularly for any access holes. Train your birds to return to the coop at evening – and be sure to close and lock it up properly.

Some other tips:

• To deter predators from accessing the interior of your coop or runs, dig a trench about 1.5 to 2 feet deep around the entire housing and bury hard ware cloth there. Determined predators can dig underground to gain access. When they attempt and fail they will normally give up and stay off your area.

• Keep compost pile far from the coop area and don't allow food leftovers to remain - clean up any food scraps that are not eaten. Remove isolated trees and other perching surfaces within reasonable meters off the flock. The less cover a predator has, the more exposed they are at being seen before attacking. This is good for the safety of your birds.

Using Modern Technologies

Some technological devises can be used to enhance other physical measure already in place. You can install solar-powered motion-detection lights to your yard to deter the predators. The light will usually give an alert when it detects any motion near the coop in the backyard. The predators will be scared and simply run away from the spotlight as they won't risk exposing themselves to attack. Garden Defense Owl is a realistic looking horned owl decoy which can be hung or perched on a pole in the yard. Predators often fear themselves they become scared at the presence of a bigger predator.

Use Guard Dogs

A well-trained dog can be used in deterring predators, both during the day and at night. Dogs are vast protectors and will keep any intruder away from the flock. They can move further away from the yard, and the scent of a dog is very disturbing to most predators.

Using Electric Fences

You can erect an electric fence around the perimeter to keep predators away. They are relatively cheap and easy to install. You can electrify these fences with little power to stun but not kill an animal. Aside from being less dangerous to people, this type of fence is more effectively keeps predators away from a flock.

About the Author

David Josephson is one of the most trusted voices in small-flock and backyard farming. He is working relentlessly promoting how to live a more sustainable life. He has written or edited a dozen of books sharing vital information and practical techniques that anyone can use on urban homesteading and backyard farming.

Made in the USA
Monee, IL
19 September 2020